Remember – green means go!

Put your pencil or crayon on the
green spot before you start to draw.

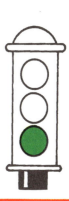

Use your crayon to draw the tracks that these
creatures have left behind.

Draw over the top of the lines.

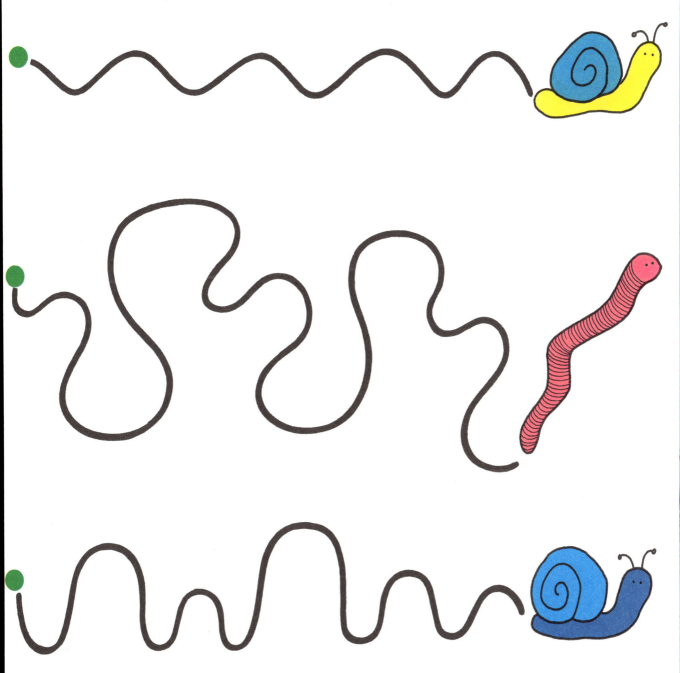

Help the man to paint his fence. Draw in all the posts.

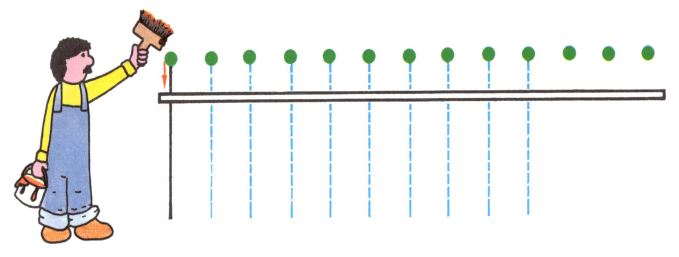

Draw the stalks on these flowers.

Draw the doors and windows on the houses.

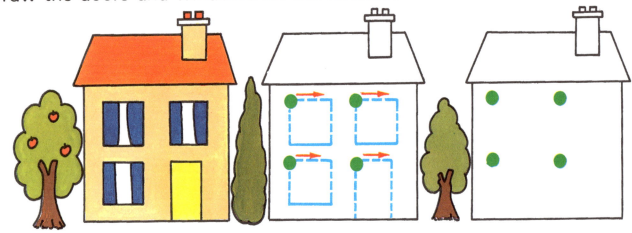

Can you draw these round shapes?
Start on the green spot and follow the dotted lines.

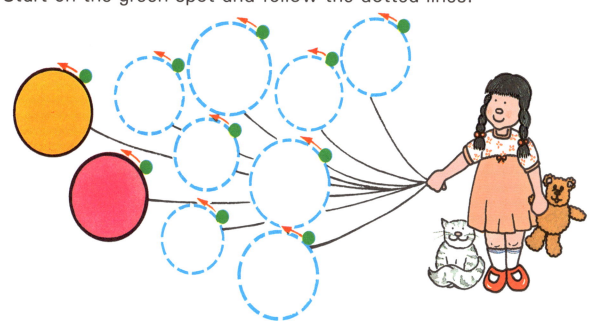

Draw the heads round these faces.

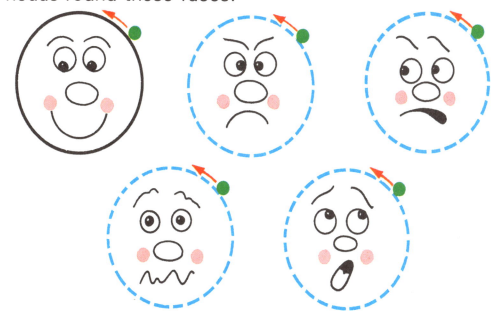

Can you draw some round shapes here?

Put the steps on the ladder so that the man can climb down.

Can you draw another ladder here?

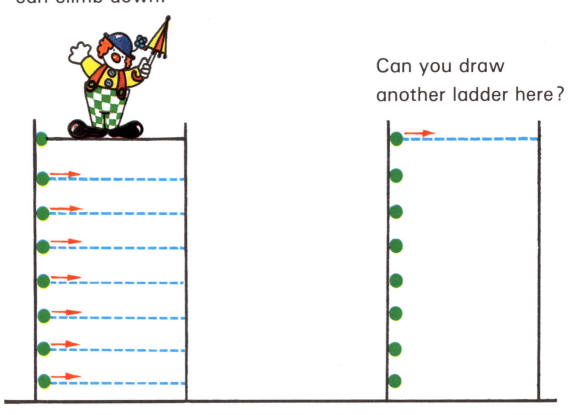

Finish drawing the teeth of the saw.

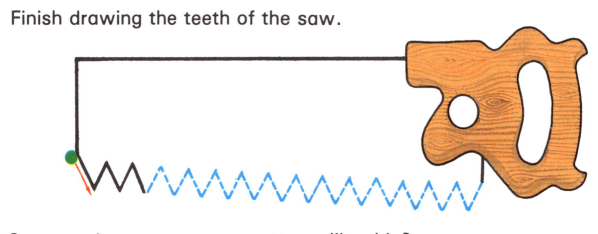

Can you draw some more patterns like this?

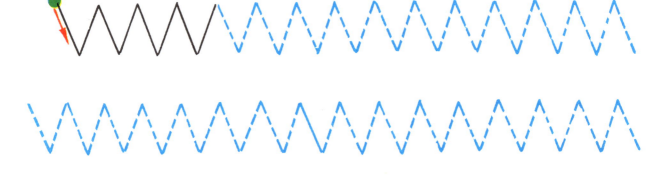

Follow with your crayon where the ball has bounced.

Draw the cups.

Follow where the girl has painted a pattern.

The top has made a pattern. Draw where it went.

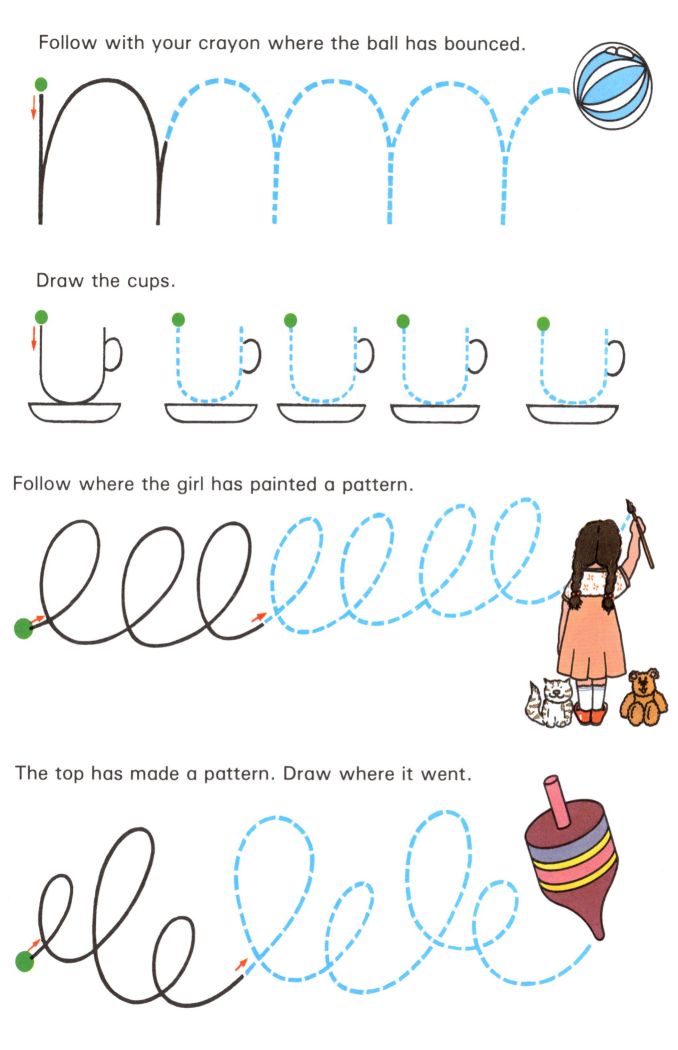

Now practise these patterns

Remember not to take your crayon off the page until you have finished each pattern or shape. Always start at the *green* spot.

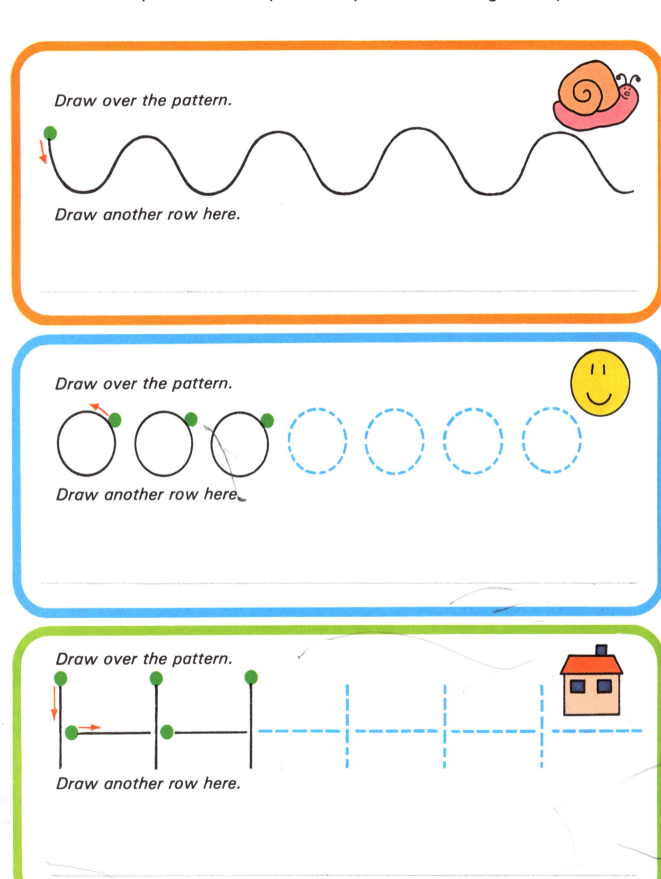

Draw over the pattern.

Draw another row here.

Draw over the pattern.

Draw another row here.

Draw over the pattern.

Draw another row here.

Draw over the pattern.

Draw another row here.

Draw over the pattern.

Draw another row here.

Draw over the pattern.

Draw another row here.

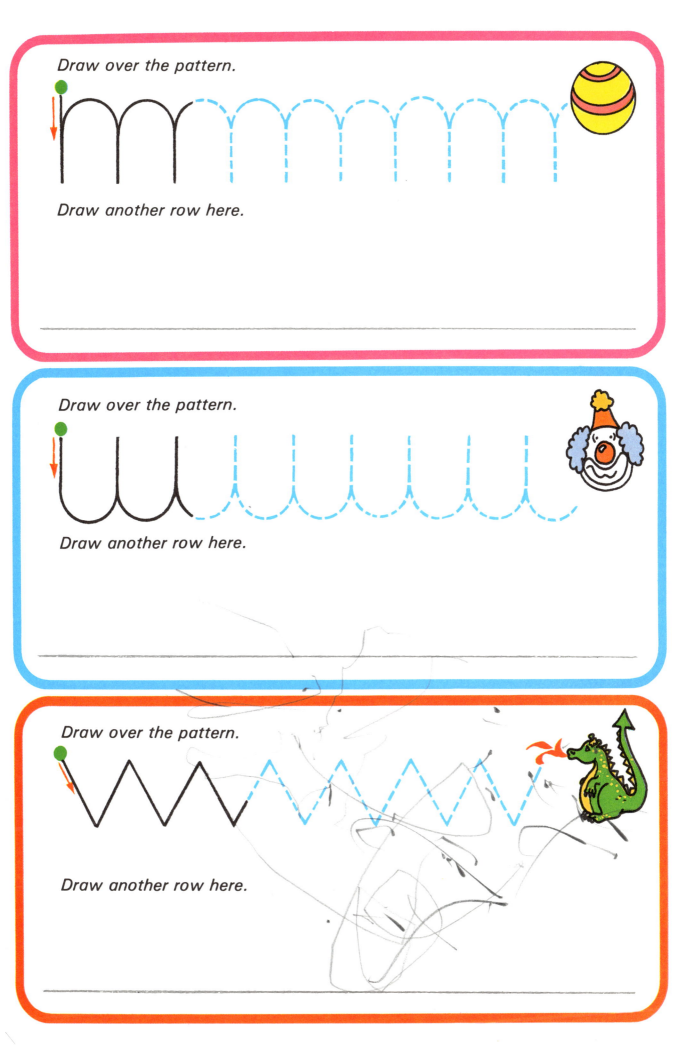

Draw over the pattern.

Draw another row here.

Draw over the pattern.

Draw another row here.

Draw over the pattern.

Draw another row here.

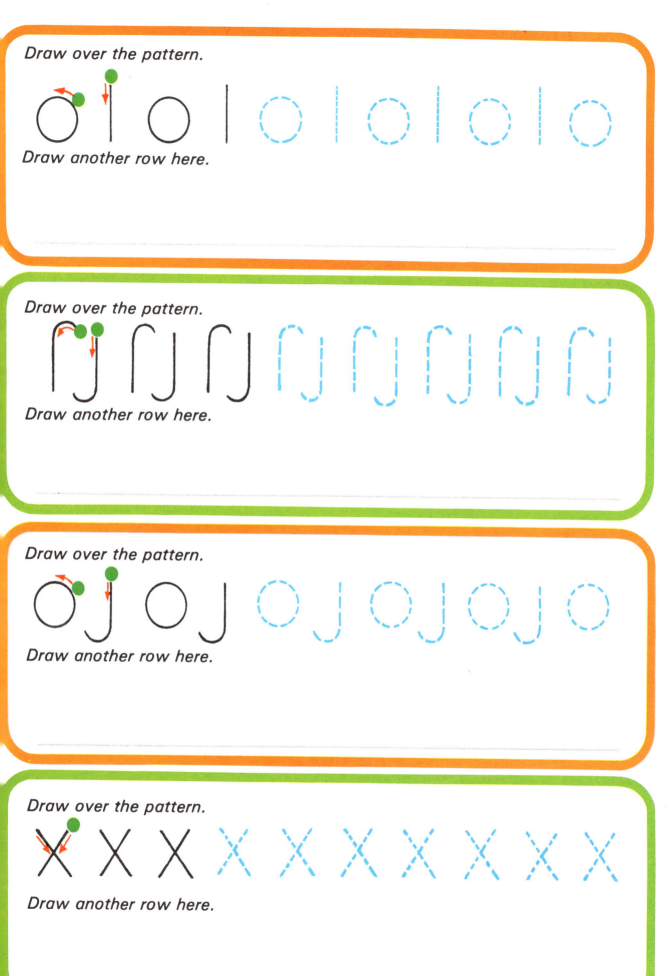

Draw over the pattern.

Draw another row here.

Draw over the pattern.

Draw another row here.

Draw over the pattern.

Draw another row here.

Draw over the pattern.

Draw another row here.

Now we can start to draw letters

Find a pencil for these pages and remember to start drawing at the *green* spot.

Draw over the letters.

C C C C C C C C

Draw over the dotted lines.

C C C C C C C C

Draw more letters here.

Draw over the letters.

O O O O O O O O

Draw over the dotted lines.

O O O O O O O O

Draw more letters here.

Draw over the letters.

a a a a a a a a

Draw over the dotted lines.

a a a a a a a a

Draw more letters here.

Draw over the letters.

d d d d d d d

Draw over the dotted lines.

d d d d d d d

Draw more letters here.

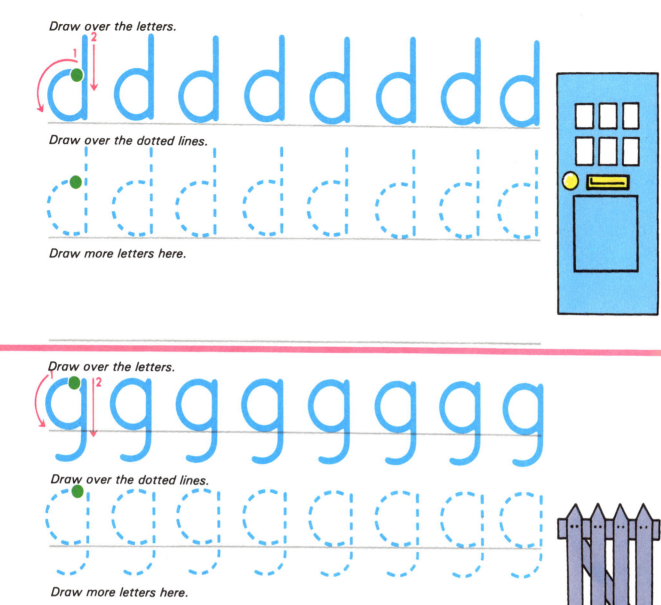

Draw over the letters.

g g g g g g g

Draw over the dotted lines.

g g g g g g g

Draw more letters here.

Draw over the letters.

q q q q q q q

Draw over the dotted lines.

q q q q q q q

Draw more letters here.

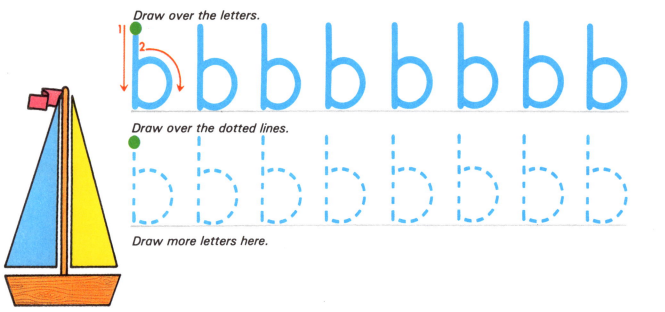

Draw over the letters.

Draw over the dotted lines.

Draw more letters here.

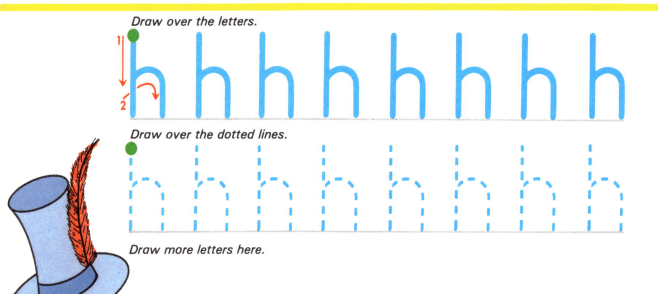

Draw over the letters.

Draw over the dotted lines.

Draw more letters here.

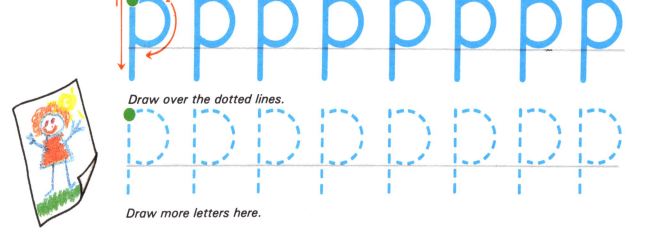

Draw over the letters.

Draw over the dotted lines.

Draw more letters here.

Draw over the letters.

Draw over the dotted lines.

Draw more letters here.

Draw over the letters.

Draw over the dotted lines.

Draw more letters here.

Draw over the letters.

Draw over the dotted lines.

Draw more letters here.

Draw over the letters.

u u u u u u u u u

Draw over the dotted lines.

Draw more letters here.

Draw over the letters.

y y y y y y y y y

Draw over the dotted lines.

Draw more letters here.

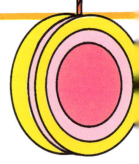

Draw over the letters.

i i i i i i i i

Draw over the dotted lines.

Draw more letters here.

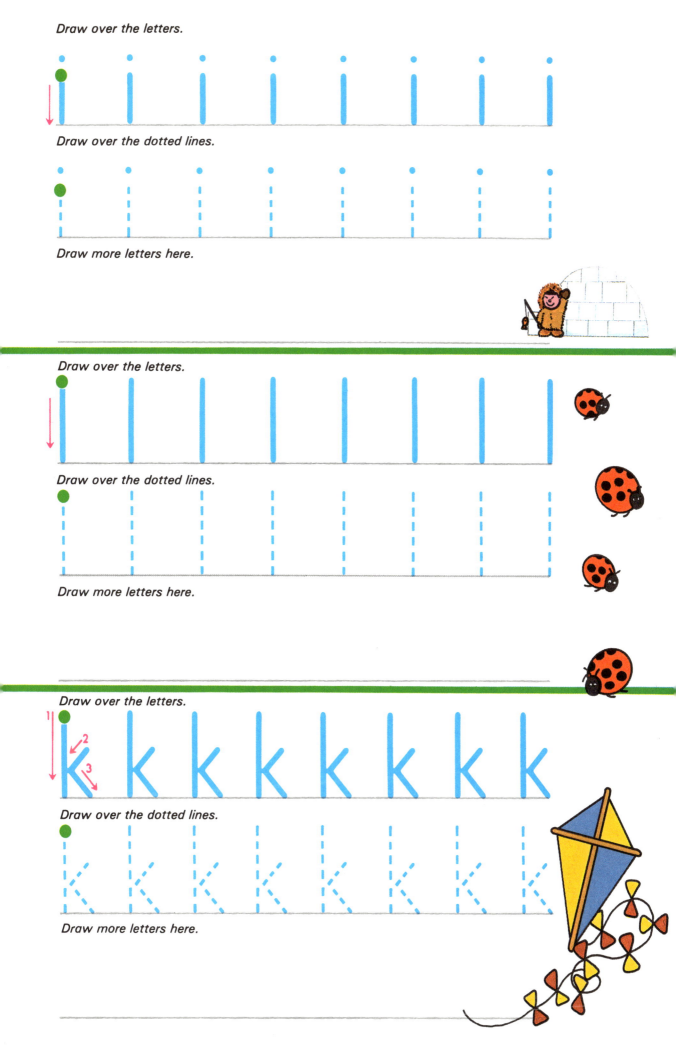

Draw over the letters.

l l l l l l l l

Draw over the dotted lines.

Draw more letters here.

Draw over the letters.

k k k k k k k k

Draw over the dotted lines.

Draw more letters here.

Draw over the letters.

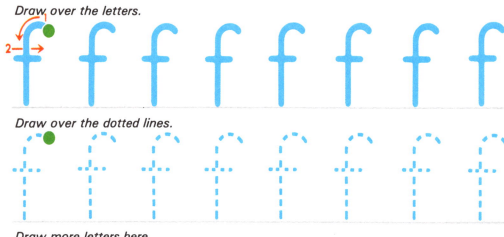

Draw over the dotted lines.

Draw more letters here.

Draw over the letters.

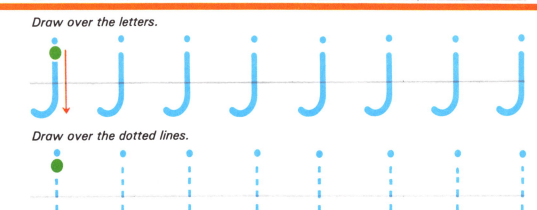

Draw over the dotted lines.

Draw more letters here.

Draw over the letters.

Draw over the dotted lines.

Draw more letters here.

Draw over the letters.

Draw over the dotted lines.

Draw more letters here.

Draw over the letters.

Draw over the dotted lines.

Draw more letters here.

Draw over the letters.

Draw over the dotted lines.

Draw more letters here.

Draw over the letters.

Draw over the dotted lines.

Draw more letters here.

Draw over the letters.

Draw over the dotted lines.

Draw more letters here.

Draw over the letters.

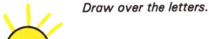

Draw over the dotted lines.

Draw more letters here.

Let's practise the letters again.

coacoacoacoa

You draw a row here.

dgqdgqdgqdgq

You draw a row here.

bhpbhpbhpbhp

You draw a row here.

nmrnmrnmrnmr

You draw a row here.

uyuyuyuyuyuyu

You draw a row here.

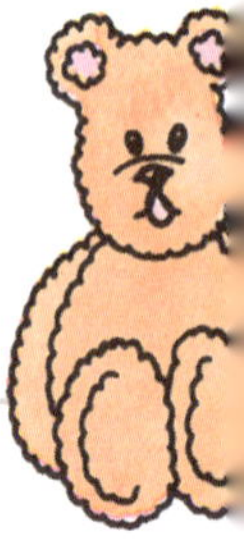

ilkilkilkilkilkilkilk

You draw a row here.

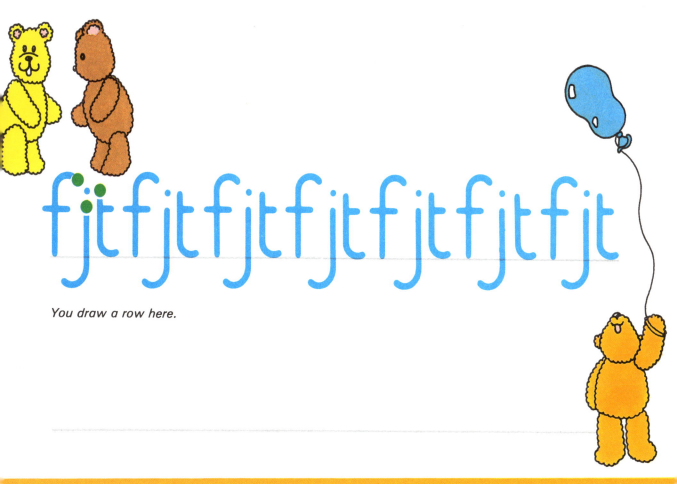

f j t f j t f j t f j t f j t f j t f j t

You draw a row here.

v w x v w x v w x v w x

You draw a row here.

z e s z e s z e s z e s z e s z e s

You draw a row here.

Here are all the letters in the right order.
This is called the *alphabet.*
Practise drawing the letters underneath.

Here is the alphabet again.

These are capital letters. We mainly use these letters at the *beginning* of important words, like names.

Practise these letters underneath.

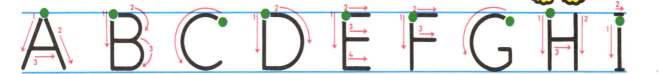

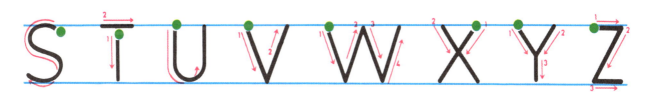

When you have practised drawing all the letter shapes you
can write your name.

Here is a name.

John Smith

Ask a grown-up to write your name below.
Use capital letters only at the *beginning*
of each word in your name.

Now *you* copy your name here.